She
Persisted

KAMALA HARRIS

— INSPIRED BY —

She Persisted

by Chelsea Clinton & Alexandra Boiger

· ·

KAMALA HARRIS

· ·

Written by
Raakhee Mirchandani

Interior illustrations by
Jessica W. Clark

PHILOMEL

PHILOMEL
An imprint of Penguin Random House LLC
1745 Broadway, New York, New York 10019

First published in the United States of America by Philomel,
an imprint of Penguin Random House LLC, 2025

Visit us online at PenguinRandomHouse.com.

Library of Congress Cataloging-in-Publication Data is available.

ISBN 9798217039586 (hardcover)
ISBN 9798217039593 (paperback)

1st Printing

Printed in the United States of America

LSCC

Edited by Talia Benamy.
Design by Ellice M. Lee.
Text set in LTC Kennerley Pro.

Dear Reader,

As Sally Ride and Marian Wright Edelman both powerfully said, "You can't be what you can't see." When Sally said that, she meant that it was hard to dream of being an astronaut, like she was, or a doctor or an athlete or anything at all if you didn't see someone like you who already had lived that dream. She especially was talking about seeing women in jobs that historically were held by men.

I wrote the first *She Persisted* and the books that came after it because I wanted young girls—and children of all genders—to see women who worked hard to live their dreams. And I wanted all of us to see examples of persistence in the face of different challenges to help inspire us in our own lives.

I'm so thrilled now to partner with a sisterhood of writers to bring longer, more in-depth versions of these stories of women's persistence and achievement to readers. I hope you enjoy these chapter books as much as I do and find them inspiring and empowering.

And remember: If anyone ever tells you no, if anyone ever says your voice isn't important or your dreams are too big, remember these women. They persisted and so should you.

Warmly,
Chelsea Clinton

She Persisted

She Persisted: WILMA MANKILLER

She Persisted: PATSY MINK

She Persisted: FLORENCE NIGHTINGALE

She Persisted: NAOMI OSAKA

She Persisted: SALLY RIDE

She Persisted: MARGARET CHASE SMITH

She Persisted: SONIA SOTOMAYOR

She Persisted: MARIA TALLCHIEF

She Persisted: DIANA TAURASI

She Persisted: HARRIET TUBMAN

She Persisted: OPRAH WINFREY

She Persisted: MALALA YOUSAFZAI

KAMALA HARRIS

TABLE OF CONTENTS

....

....

Truth to Power

B efore the iconic pearls and pantsuits—and before groundbreaking runs for office that would change American history and politics— Kamala Devi Harris was a little girl in California, sitting in a stroller while her parents protested in support of civil rights and freedom. Kamala learned from a very early age the importance of using your voice to spark change. She saw first-hand the power people have when they come together in support of something they believe in.

Kamala Harris was born on October 20, 1964, in Oakland, California, to Shyamala Gopalan Harris and Donald Harris. It was the same year that the Civil Rights Act was passed. The Civil Rights Act is a law that aims to make sure people cannot be discriminated against because of their race, color, religion, sex, or national origin, including in the workplace.

Kamala's mother, Shyamala, was an Indian immigrant who moved to California for graduate school. She was a brilliant student, and she was accepted to the University of California, Berkeley, to study nutrition and endocrinology. She would later become a very respected breast cancer researcher. (Endocrinology is the study of the endocrine system. The endocrine system controls the hormones in your body, which help make your body work properly.)

Kamala's father, Donald, was also a brilliant student. Born in Jamaica in 1938, he immigrated to America to attend UC Berkeley, too. He studied economics and later taught that subject at Stanford University. Shyamala and Donald met during a time in American history when many people were protesting against war and racial injustice. Both Donald and Shyamala cared deeply about these causes and the way Black Americans were being treated, and they spent their time learning, reading, and talking to other people who felt similarly to them, and organizing against things they thought were unfair and unjust.

The two met and bonded over their shared values and vision for what America—and their community—could be. And after they got married and had children, they made sure their daughters, Kamala and her younger sister, Maya, were a part of that fight, too.

Like her parents, Kamala knew what was fair and unfair. And when things felt wrong to her, she spoke up and did something about it.

In kindergarten, when a bully flung her friend Stacey's clay art project to the floor, little Kamala stood up for her friend. The bully was so mad, he hit Kamala on the head. She still has a scar over one eye from that day. But Kamala knew that being an upstander, not a bystander, was important. An upstander is a person who chooses to support someone who is being harmed by standing up for them, not just watching.

"I was born a Black child in America, the

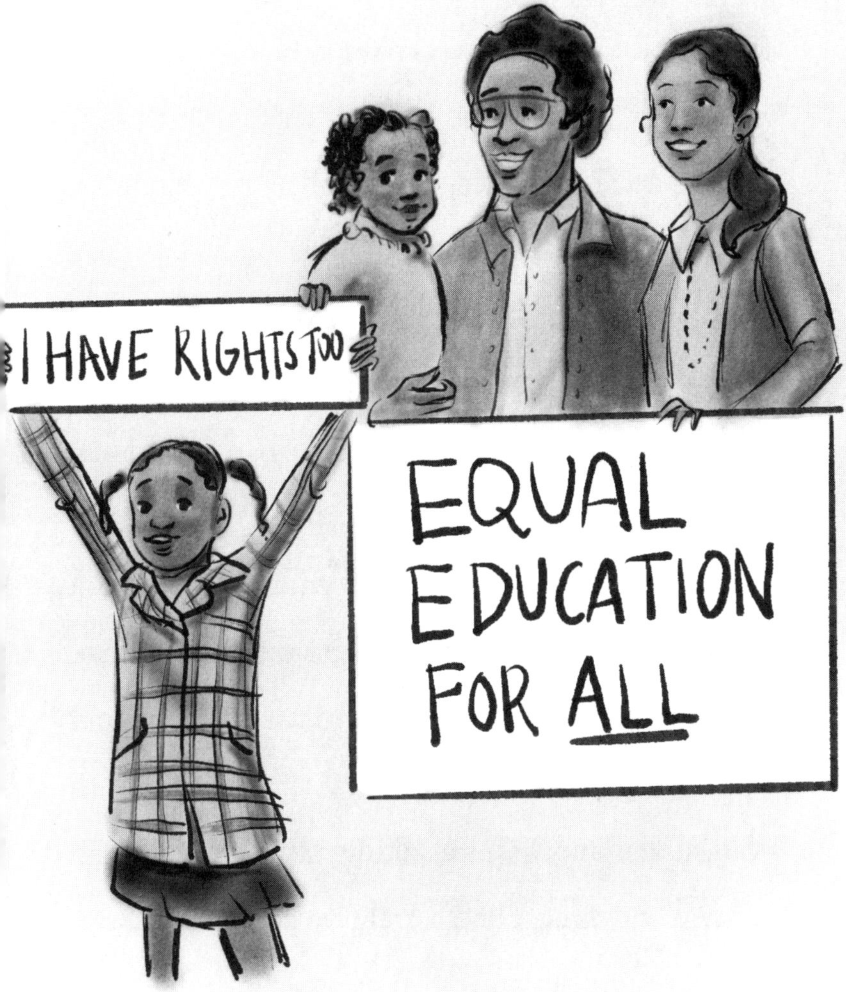
I HAVE RIGHTS TOO
EQUAL EDUCATION FOR ALL

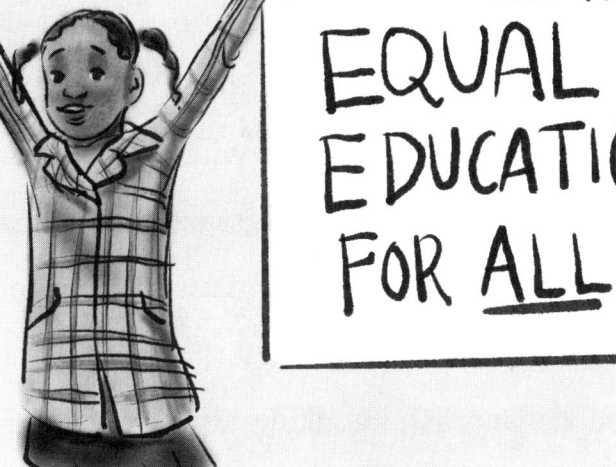

child of parents who were marching and shouting, just like all the folks who have been marching and shouting," Kamala said later in her life. "From my childhood, I was there in a stroller in the streets, marching. It's just what I do. It's what I believe in. I don't know any other way."

Music was also a big part of the Harris household. Kamala's mom liked gospel, and she sang along to Aretha Franklin and the Edwin Hawkins Singers, especially when she cooked, something she loved to do. She would make okra, sometimes in an Indian style, with turmeric and mustard seeds, and sometimes as a gumbo with soul food flavoring, by adding dried shrimp and sausage. Shyamala had a great voice and had even won a singing award when she was in India. And as Shyamala sang at home, Kamala would join in, singing and dancing to Aretha's version of Nina Simone's "To Be Young, Gifted and Black." Donald loved jazz and filled the air with tunes from Thelonious Monk, John Coltrane, and Miles Davis.

Like Shyamala, Kamala's maternal grandparents—her mother's parents—believed in participating in political and social change in their community. Her grandmother, Rajam Gopalan, took care of women in her village and educated them about women's health issues. She also was known to speak up about abuse against women and in support of women's healthcare, even if it meant calling their husbands and telling them to "shape up." Kamala's grandfather, P. V. Gopalan, was part of India's independence movement and became a senior diplomat in the Indian government.

Rajam and P. V. even moved to Zambia for a time to help settle refugees. Serving people and their communities was a big part of the Gopalan family's values, ones that would shape Kamala's life for decades to come.

"My mother inherited my grandmother's strength and courage. People who knew them knew not to mess with either. And from both of my grandparents, my mother developed a keen political consciousness. She was conscious of history, conscious of struggle, and conscious of inequities," Kamala said. "She was born with a sense of justice imprinted on her soul."

When Kamala was seven years old and Maya was just a toddler, their parents got divorced. The girls lived with their mother in East Bay near San Francisco and spent weekends and summers with their father in Palo Alto, also in the Bay Area. They visited their father's family in Jamaica and their mother's family in India. The Harris girls were surrounded by friends, relatives, and chosen family, who built their strong sense of identity.

At Thousand Oaks Elementary School, Kamala was in Mrs. Wilson's first-grade classroom. It wasn't until years later that Kamala learned her school was part of a national experiment in desegregation. Desegregation meant that kids from Kamala's mostly working-class Black neighborhood took the bus to go to school with kids in wealthier, white neighborhoods—and sometimes the other way around—in an effort to make the school populations more diverse. After school, while Shyamala was still at the lab working on important research, the Harris sisters would head over to the Sheltons' house for an after-school program. The warm home—with posters of Frederick Douglass, Sojourner Truth, and Harriet Tubman on the walls—left a lasting impact on Kamala. Mrs. Shelton was a mother figure to Kamala, too.

Once, Kamala spent an afternoon baking lemon bars. They looked picture perfect, and she couldn't wait to show them off. She proudly brought them over to share with her mom, Mrs. Shelton, and another neighborhood friend who they called Aunt Bea. They were having tea together. But Kamala realized something wasn't right when Mrs. Shelton's lips puckered.

"Mmmm, honey," Mrs. Shelton said. "That's delicious . . . maybe a little too much salt . . . but really delicious." Kamala had mistakenly used salt instead of sugar! But instead of feeling like a failure, Kamala knew she had done a great job; she had just made a mistake. And her confidence continued to grow.

Kamala's bond with her mother was also growing stronger every day. Shyamala's strength, leadership, toughness, and work ethic inspired her daughters. She was a mama on a mission: to raise two confident and proud Black daughters and to help end breast cancer.

CHAPTER 2

Shyamala and the Girls

K amala learned to play the piano down the street at Mrs. Jones's house and played chess at Aunt Mary and Uncle Sherman's. On Saturdays, the girls did their chores, and on Sundays, they went to church with Mrs. Shelton. The community showed up for Shyamala, and the girls loved their community right back. But Kamala's favorite night of the week was Thursday, when she went to Rainbow Sign.

Rainbow Sign was a Black cultural center and a place the trio—Shyamala, Kamala, and Maya—always felt at home. Congresswoman Shirley Chisholm visited Rainbow Sign when she was exploring a run for president. Writers such as Alice Walker and Maya Angelou did readings at the center, and singer Nina Simone performed there when Kamala was seven years old. Kamala learned a lot in that space, especially how cool it was to be smart, ambitious, and artsy. Excellence was everywhere, and Kamala's own ambitions were growing, too.

The kitchen was an important place in Kamala's home. It was where a lot of family bonding took place. Sometimes Shyamala would make the girls a "smorgasbord," using a cookie cutter to make bread into fun shapes and laying out condiments and leftovers to stick between the bread. It was a really fun way to make leftovers exciting! The girls also had "unbirthday" parties. If someone needed a pick-me-up—or if it had been a gloomy week—the family would have unbirthday cake and unbirthday gifts. Shyamala even let her daughters pick the color of her new car! The girls picked yellow, which made it easy to spot their Dodge Dart in parking lots.

But things were about to change dramatically for the Harris girls. Shyamala got a new job, and when Kamala was twelve years old, the family had to move to Montréal, Canada. It was hard to leave California and the Bay Area, home to so many important Black leaders. It was hard to leave Rainbow Sign and the aunties and uncles from the neighborhood. But, like the flower she was named after—Kamala means *lotus* in Sanskrit— Kamala Harris could bloom anywhere.

Living in Montréal was an adjustment. But it's also where Kamala got her first taste of community organizing. One day, she and Maya organized a protest in front of their apartment building. The kids who lived there wanted to play soccer on the lawn, but building rules didn't allow for that. All those years of watching folks stand up for what they believed in—and knowing the power of coming together to get something done—worked. The building changed the rules, and Kamala, Maya, and their friends were able to use the lawn for soccer!

The girls visited California during vacations and summers. They stayed with their dad and with Mrs. Shelton. For the rest of the year, they

settled in and got used to Canadian life, though Kamala missed where she grew up. She missed America.

"What I hadn't gotten used to was the feeling of being homesick for my country. I felt this constant sense of yearning to be back home. There was no question in my mind I'd return home for college," she said.

In high school Kamala started thinking more seriously about her future. She thought about who she wanted to be and looked to the women around her for inspiration. She was surrounded by people—including many women—who were successful in their respective careers, and that inspired her to dream big, too. Kamala valued being able to help and being the one people relied on when they needed a solution. The more she thought about it, the more she realized that being a lawyer was something she wanted to pursue.

"I cared a lot about fairness, and I saw the law as a tool that can help make things fair," she said. "But I think what most drew me to the profession was the way people around me trusted and relied on lawyers."

And so, in 1982, Kamala Harris started college at Howard University, an HBCU. HBCUs, or Historically Black Colleges and Universities, are institutions that were created to educate African American students before the Civil Rights Act of 1964, when many universities were segregated and wouldn't allow Black students to attend.

Settling in at Howard was easy. Kamala felt at home right away. She particularly liked hanging out on the Yard, a grassy area right in the middle of campus. It was a great place to watch people practicing step routines, musicians playing their instruments, and students gathering, talking, connecting, and being in community.

"Every signal told students that we could

be anything—that we were young, gifted, and Black, and we shouldn't let anything get in the way of our success," Kamala said about her alma mater. "The campus was a place where you didn't have to be confined to the box of another person's choosing. At Howard, you could come as you were and leave as the person you aspired to be."

Howard is also where Kamala Harris ran for office the very first time. In her first year at school, Kamala ran to be freshman class representative of the Liberal Arts Student Council. It was her first campaign, and she ran against a tough opponent, Shelley Young, and won. Kamala also got involved by competing on the debate team, chairing the economics society, and pledging Alpha Kappa Alpha, a sorority that is still important to her today. Always the daughter of

Shyamala and Donald, Kamala stayed rooted in her strong sense of social justice. On weekends, she would protest apartheid, an unjust system of government in South Africa that prevented Black South Africans from being treated as equal members of their society.

Kamala made sure she took advantage of every opportunity she had while at Howard. And since Howard was located in Washington, DC, she was surrounded by the highest levels of the United States government. Kamala interned at the Federal Trade Commission and did research at the National Archives. She was also a tour guide at the Bureau of Engraving and Printing. One summer, she got a job interning for California senator Alan Cranston.

Kamala loved going to the Capitol building

for work, even if she just sorted mail sometimes. But she was even more taken by the Supreme Court building across the street, with the words EQUAL JUSTICE UNDER LAW emblazoned above the entrance. Being in the middle of it all—and seeing the ways the law and government could help people—struck a chord in her heart.

More than three decades after interning for Senator Cranston, Kamala was elected to that same Senate seat by the people of California. Dreams are powerful, important things, especially when they are powered by hard work, grit, and determination.

CHAPTER 3

Young, Gifted, and Black

After college, Kamala headed home to Oakland and attended the University of California Hastings College of the Law.

While she was there, she ran her second campaign and was elected president of the Black Law Students Association. When she noticed that Black students were having a harder time finding jobs than white students, Kamala took action. She knew she had the chance to change the way things were working and make the situation more fair for all students. Motivated by the need to make things better, she called the managing partners at major law firms and asked them to send recruiters and representatives to a job fair.

It was this kind of problem-solving that made Kamala stand out.

Soon it was time for Kamala to enter the working world. All she needed to do was take the bar exam. The bar exam is the last step in becoming a licensed, practicing lawyer in America. She finished law school in 1989 and took the bar exam that summer. She even had a job lined up as deputy district attorney, an opportunity she earned by interning at the district attorney's office the summer before. But things didn't go as planned.

The first time she took the bar exam, Kamala failed it. She didn't put in the work to study for the test, and it showed. She felt like she wasn't good enough or smart enough. She still was able to keep her job, though they had to give her different things to do so that she could have time to study to retake the test.

Embarrassed by her failure, Kamala knew what she had to do. And despite how she felt, she kept her head up, studied hard, and persisted. She passed her bar exam on her second try and learned a valuable lesson: that she had to put in her full effort, every time, in everything she did.

Working at the district attorney's office, also called the DA's office, was a dream come true for Kamala. But her friends and family didn't feel exactly the same way. The DA, who serves as the

prosecutor in courtrooms, is a lawyer who represents the state and the people of the area they work in. Their role is to get justice on behalf of society against people accused of crimes. But the legal system isn't always fair to certain communities, and Kamala knew that some prosecutors had used the power of their offices against people of color. She also knew that other prosecutors, as well as other people with political power, had done work to help people of color. Robert F. Kennedy, when he was the US attorney general in the 1960s, had sent protection for the Freedom Riders, a group of people trying to end discrimination in the South. He also sent US marshals to protect James Meredith, the first Black student to attend the University of Mississippi.

Kamala was convinced of the value of

changing the system from the inside. She believed the law could—and should—provide equal protection and justice for all people. And she wanted to be a change agent.

Looking back at this decision, she later said: "One of my mother's favorite sayings was, 'Don't let anybody tell you who you are. You tell them who you are.' And so I did. I knew part of making change was what I'd seen all my life, surrounded by adults shouting and marching and demanding justice from the outside. But I also knew there was an important role on the inside, sitting at the table where the decisions were being made. When activists came marching and banging on the doors, I wanted to be on the other side to let them in."

In court, every time she stepped up to the

podium to speak, she started with, "Kamala Harris, for the people." This statement became a guiding light for Kamala as she did the grueling, difficult work of being a prosecutor. She thought about the people she was representing—the citizens of the community and the victims, those who had been wronged and deserved justice. She knew people who had broken the law should suffer the consequences of their actions, but she also wanted to make sure that the consequences fit the crime.

The lessons Kamala had learned from her mother and Rainbow Sign, from the Howard Yard and Mrs. Shelton, helped her see things from her own perspective and make her own mark for the better. And it was working. In 1998 she was asked to join the San Francisco district attorney's office. Kamala wasn't sure what to say, because the San Francisco office didn't have a great reputation. She decided to take the job, but it was a difficult experience. After eighteen months, she was recruited for a different job, this time with the San Francisco city attorney's office. In this job, Kamala worked to make things better for young people who had faced abuse. She spent two years there.

"My vision of a progressive prosecutor was someone who used the power of the office with a sense of fairness, perspective, and experience, someone who was clear about the need to hold serious criminals accountable and who understood that the best way to create safe communities was to prevent crime in the first place," she said.

Kamala couldn't shake the feeling that

becoming the district attorney herself, the top prosecutor in the whole office, was what she needed to do to have the most impact. She knew what she wanted to change about the DA's office and the way things were getting done, but if she wasn't the boss, she wouldn't be able to accomplish those goals. But that top job was an elected position, which meant that getting it would require her to run a political campaign in a very public election. And her opponent would be her former boss. She had no experience running a campaign outside of a school setting, or raising the money she would need to run for office, but she knew it was now or never.

California Campaigns

Campaigning is an important part of running for office. Campaigning is when you organize around achieving a particular goal. In this case, the goal was to get enough votes to win the election. Campaigning also means talking to potential voters and meeting as many people as possible to let them know who you are, what you stand for, and what your plans would be if you were to be elected.

Kamala was clear on what her plans would be. Having worked in the DA's office before, she knew she wanted to run it in a more professional way. But she also knew she wanted to make sure there were programs in place to lift people up. She believed that preventing crime—and making sure people had opportunities to be successful—would change both communities and lives.

Kamala campaigned with her mother and sister. She campaigned with friends and, of course, volunteers. Volunteering for a campaign—or a cause you care about—is a good way to get involved in your community. Volunteers call voters, stuff envelopes for campaign mailers, and go door-to-door to chat with community members about the candidate they are supporting and why.

Kamala campaigned everywhere, from grocery stores to community centers, neighborhoods, and private homes.

"If you think running for office sounds glamorous, I wish you could have seen me striding through the parking lot with an ironing board under my arm. I remember the kids who would look curiously at the ironing board and point, and the moms who would hustle them past," she said. "I couldn't blame them. I must have looked out of place—if not totally out of my mind. But an ironing board makes for the perfect standing desk."

Kamala was asking people for their support and their votes. And they, in turn, wanted to know more about her as a person.

Voting is an important American right. Originally, according to the Constitution (written

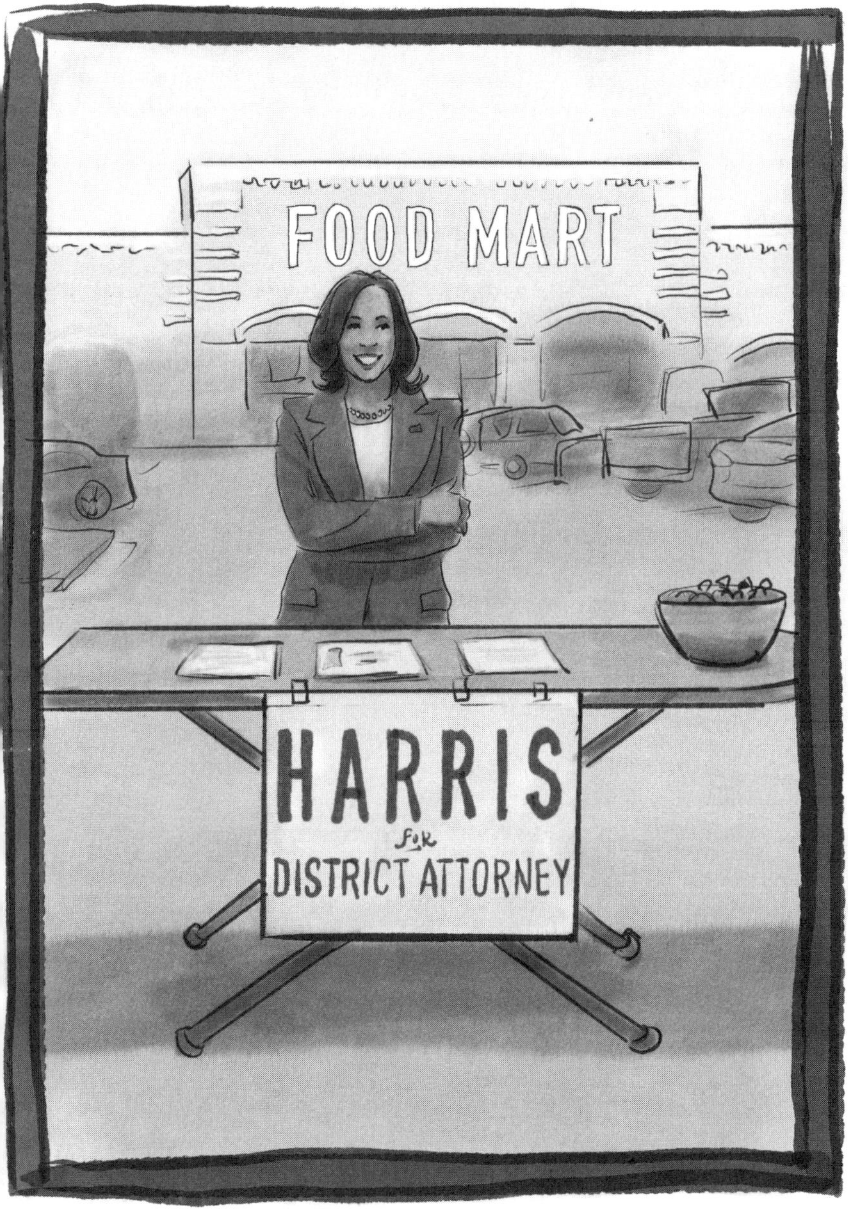
FOOD MART
HARRIS
FOR
DISTRICT ATTORNEY

in 1787), only white males over the age of twenty-one who owned property could vote. In 1870 the Fifteenth Amendment to the Constitution was ratified, officially protecting the rights of all male citizens to vote, regardless of race. But that didn't stop certain states from making it hard for Black men to cast their votes, through tactics like poll taxes, literacy tests, and even violence. Women didn't have the right to vote till 1920, when the Nineteenth Amendment was ratified. Native Americans didn't gain the right to vote in federal elections until 1924. Even after those advancements, women from communities of color continued to face barriers to voting. In 1965 President Lyndon B. Johnson signed the Voting Rights Act, one of the most successful civil rights protections in US history. This meant that no one could be denied the right to vote based on their race.

"It is wrong, deadly wrong, to deny any of your fellow Americans the right to vote in this country," President Johnson said. "There is no issue of states' rights or national rights, there is only the struggle for human rights."

In 2003, after a hard-fought campaign, Kamala Harris earned the votes she needed. She was elected as San Francisco district attorney, the first woman and the first person of color to be elected to this role. She gave her victory speech as Queen's song "We Are the Champions" played loudly for everyone to hear. She was sworn in to her role in 2004, with her mother by her side. Shyamala was so proud of her daughter, and Kamala knew it. One man even brought his two young daughters to the inauguration so they could see what was possible for them.

Then it was time to do the work.

In 2005 Kamala made good on one of her campaign promises. She started Back on Track, a program that helped people charged with low-level, nonviolent crimes get back on their feet. If they went to school, got counseling, and participated in community service, their charges would be dropped, and they would have a clean criminal record. Kamala believed in redemption: the idea that you could earn your way back from a mistake by serving your time and doing the right thing going forward.

Not everyone believed in this program, and many people pushed back. But Kamala persisted. She wanted to make a real difference, and she wanted to prove that her idea could work. And it did. Back on Track was so successful that other states and communities created their own versions of the program. Even President Barack

Obama created something similar when he was in the White House!

Kamala also had to fight for her efforts to bring down truancy. Truancy is when students skip school without a good reason. She believed that people who didn't finish school were more likely to get involved in crimes. It was something she had noticed as a prosecutor, and she wanted to try to fix it.

Kamala wanted to do this by getting families and students the support they needed to keep kids in school. She also put laws in place that could fine or jail parents if their kids' truancy continued to be a problem. Some people thought it wasn't the government's place to be involved in school and family issues. Others thought the families who were being impacted by the rules were already struggling and this only added to their burdens. But Kamala believed that these laws were helping to prevent future crimes by strengthening communities and community members.

Things got very difficult for Kamala in 2008, when her mother was diagnosed with cancer. The day Kamala got that news was one of the worst days of her life. In 2009, after spending time with her daughters and friends, and after a visit from her brother from India, Shyamala Gopalan Harris passed away.

It was a painful time for Kamala, but her mother's fighting spirit lived in her, too. She had just gotten into the race for attorney general of all of California, and she wanted to win. A state attorney general serves as an advisor to the leaders of the state on legal matters, and this job would allow her to fight on behalf of Californians in a bigger way. In 2010, Kamala Harris became the first woman and the first person of color to be elected attorney general of California.

CHAPTER 5

Kamala Harris, for the People

B efore she could even settle into her new role as attorney general, Kamala had to fight on behalf of the people of California in a major way. A couple of years earlier, in 2008, America had gone through some really tough times, and many Americans had lost their jobs and could no longer afford to stay in their homes. It was scary for a lot of families, and millions of Americans were out of work. The people of California were hit hard, and big banks were putting pressure on people to pay up (something that they couldn't do without jobs and salaries) or leave their homes.

Kamala knew the banks had taken advantage of Americans. She wanted justice. Families were suffering and, as attorney general, she had the power to get results. She had been told the banks would give Californians somewhere between $2 billion and $4 billion. But Kamala felt they deserved more. After tough negotiations, she helped get $18 billion for the people of her state.

"Americans are a hardworking bunch," Kamala said. "We pride ourselves on our work ethic. And for generations, most of us have been raised to believe that there are few things more honorable than putting in an honest day's work to take care of our family."

Also in 2008, when Barack Obama was elected president, Californians voted to pass Proposition 8. This was an amendment to the California constitution that took away the right of same-sex couples to marry. The only way to get that right back was to bring it to court, which took a very long time. A federal court decided that Proposition 8 shouldn't be allowed to stand because it went against the Constitution, but even then, people who supported it tried to keep it in place. Finally, in 2013, after going all the way to the Supreme Court, Proposition 8 was officially taken down. After years of advocacy, legal action, and hard work, marriage equality was legal again in California. Through it all, as California's attorney general, Kamala refused to defend Proposition 8.

The people who had brought the case to the courts, Kris Perry and Sandy Stier, were the first same-sex couple to get married in California after Proposition 8 was overturned. Kamala Harris performed the ceremony, and history was made. Hundreds of couples across California were also married that day. People celebrated in the streets waving rainbow flags, and joy filled the air.

"Today we witness not only the joining of Kris and Sandy, but the realization of their dream—marriage . . . By joining the case against Proposition 8, they represented thousands of couples like themselves in the fight for marriage equality. Through ups and downs, the struggles and triumphs, they came out victorious," Kamala said.

A year later, in 2014, Kamala got married, too. She had met Doug Emhoff, who was also a

lawyer, through a friend, and they quickly fell in love. Her sister, Maya, officiated the ceremony, and her niece Meena read a piece that had been written by the great writer and civil rights activist Maya Angelou. They honored both Kamala's Indian heritage and Doug's Jewish heritage at the ceremony with traditions from both cultures. Doug's kids from his first marriage, Ella and Cole, called their stepmother Momala.

One of the things the family loves doing together as often as possible is Sunday dinner. Cole picks the music and sets the table, Ella makes beautiful desserts, and Doug chops onions. Kamala makes the main dish—spaghetti Bolognese, Indian biryani, chickpeas with feta and herbs from her garden, fish tacos, homemade pizzas, or other recipes the family enjoys. This meal is a time for connection and spending time with each other. Even when the family is busy, or people are traveling, it's a tradition that gets prioritized.

In 2015 longtime California senator Barbara

Boxer announced that she would not be seeking reelection in 2016. Kamala knew that a Senate seat would allow her to do even more work on behalf of the people of California. As a senator, she'd be able to make an impact on so many of the issues she cared about: criminal justice reform, climate change, support for families and immigrant communities, and the housing problems that still remained after the 2008 crisis. Kamala knew that, with her voice in the rooms where important decisions were being made about America's future, she could make an even bigger difference. She decided to run for the Senate.

The campaign was fierce, and Kamala's team traveled across the state in a bus they nicknamed "Kamoji" because of the Kamala cartoon emblazoned on the back. She had come a long way from using an ironing board as a standing desk in the grocery store parking lot, but Kamala knew that the way to win a campaign was still the same: meet the people and show them who you are and what you stand for.

Kamala won her Senate election in November 2016, the same year Donald Trump was elected president. She was the second Black woman and the first South Asian woman to serve in the Senate. And in her first speech as a senator, on February 16, 2017, she started off with a nod to her hero: "Above all, I rise today with a sense of gratitude for all those upon whose shoulders we stand. For me, it starts with my mother, Shyamala Harris."

....

CHAPTER 6

The First but Not the Last

Kamala Harris has had many firsts in her career.

She is a trailblazer, often holding positions and elected offices that women, Black women, and South Asian women had never held before. Her confidence, determination, and willingness to serve the people of California have created pathways for other women from communities of color to follow in her footsteps.

"It's our job to stand up for those who are not at the table where life-altering decisions are made," she said. "Not just those people who look like us. Not just those who need what we need. Not just those who have gained an audience with us. Our duty is to improve the human condition—in every way we can, for everyone who needs it."

As senator, something Kamala Harris was well-known for was asking tough questions during Senate committee hearings. Hearings are how Senate committees—groups of senators assigned to a specific topic or issue—gather information. As a former prosecutor, she knew how important getting accurate information was. She was gaining attention on a national level now, and her influence was spreading beyond her home state.

In January 2019 Kamala launched her own campaign for president of the United States. She was going to run against President Trump, who was seeking a second term. She launched her campaign in Oakland, California, where she was born. Crowds gathered to hear her speak, and many Americans were energized by her. But by June, twenty candidates had announced their intentions to become the Democratic nominee and run for president. Getting nominated wasn't going to be simple, but Kamala wasn't afraid of doing hard things, especially if she believed in them.

Running for office—especially president—is really expensive. And Kamala's campaign was having trouble getting the donations needed to continue such a pricey campaign. She ended up dropping out of the presidential race in December.

It wasn't an easy decision, but even though the
campaign didn't go as planned, Kamala had done
her best. And then in August 2020, because her
track record as district attorney, attorney general,

and senator were so well-known, Joe Biden, who had become the official Democratic nominee, announced that Kamala would be his running mate for vice president. And in true Kamala fashion, it was another first for her list: the first woman of color to run for vice president of the United States.

Kamala, in her trademark Converse sneakers, pearl necklace, and pantsuit, hit the campaign trail. And while parts of campaigning felt familiar, this was a bigger race than she'd ever run before. On November 7, 2020, Joe Biden and Kamala Harris won the election. The American people had spoken, and Kamala became the first female vice president in American history.

"While I may be the first woman in this office," she said, "I will not be the last, because every little girl watching tonight sees that this is a country of possibilities."

President Biden and Vice President Harris served the American people together for four years. And when it was time for new elections in 2024, President Biden and Kamala Harris ran together again, talking about all that they had accomplished for the American people. Then President Biden decided that he would no longer run for reelection and dropped out of the race. It's uncommon in American history for a sitting president to not run for reelection or to drop out of a race that they've already entered. But President Biden immediately endorsed Vice President Harris to be the next president; she had his support and his vote. In August 2024 Kamala received enough support to be the Democratic party's official nominee for president of the United States. She would face former President Trump, who was running again, at the polls.

On August 19, 2024, the Democratic National Convention, also known as the DNC, kicked off in Chicago, Illinois. The DNC and Republican National Convention are presidential nominating conventions, in which the two major US political parties formally select the candidate who will represent them on the ballot during the November election. In 2016, former Secretary of State Hillary Clinton became the first woman ever to be the presidential nominee of a major US party. When that had happened, people talked about how she had put cracks in the glass ceiling, which was another way of saying that she had broken barriers. Now, in 2024, Kamala was the first woman of color to earn this honor.

A lot of people spoke at the DNC, includ-ing President Biden and former presidents Bill Clinton and Barack Obama. Activists, senators, governors, and even Kamala's great-nieces gave speeches. Stacey, her friend from kindergarten, told the story about her broken art project! Talk show host Oprah Winfrey, former First Lady Michelle Obama, and former Secretary of State Hillary Clinton gave speeches, too.

In her speech, Hillary Clinton said, "Together we've put a lot of cracks in the highest, hardest glass ceiling. And tonight, tonight's so close to breaking through once and for all . . . And you know what? On the other side of that glass ceil-ing is Kamala Harris raising her hand and taking the oath of office as our forty-seventh president of the United States. Because, my friends, when a barrier falls for one of us, it falls, it falls and clears the way for all of us."

Kamala accepted the historic nomination on August 22, 2024. In her speech that night, she talked about so many people who had touched her life: her mother, Mrs. Shelton, and the uncles and aunties from the neighborhood—the Harrises' chosen family. She talked about why she wanted to be president and about her experiences as a prosecutor, standing up for the people of California.

"And so, on behalf of the people, on behalf of every American, regardless of party, race, gender, or the language your grandmother speaks . . . On behalf of my mother, and everyone who has ever set out on their own unlikely journey . . . On behalf of Americans like the people I grew up with—people who work hard, chase their dreams, and look out for one another . . . On behalf of everyone whose story could only be written in the greatest nation on Earth, I accept your nomination to be president of the United States of America," she said.

Kamala hit the campaign trail again, this time for the highest office in the country. She had chosen Minnesota governor Tim Walz as her running mate, and he hit the trail, too. They traveled to small towns and big cities to meet voters, holding large rallies and smaller, more intimate events. They met as many Americans as they could, telling people who they were and about their vision for America's future. Hundreds of thousands of volunteers donated their time and energy to help the Harris-Walz campaign by raising money,

making phone calls, knocking on doors, hosting debate watch parties, and more.

Throughout her life, Kamala had witnessed racism against her mother. Sometimes people made hurtful assumptions or treated her mother poorly and with disrespect because of her Indian accent. Kamala, too, faced this kind of ugly disrespect with her own name. People, including elected officials, purposely mispronounced her name as a way to make fun of her or make her feel like she didn't belong. But Kamala knew who she was and what she stood for. She had a goal in front of her, and she wasn't going to be distracted by bullying.

On Tuesday, November 5, 2024, it was time for the American people to vote for the candidate they thought would be the best next president. But the election didn't go the way Kamala had hoped. Despite her best efforts and campaigning, the Harris-Walz ticket wasn't successful. President Trump had won the election; the American people had spoken.

With her head held high, Vice President Harris called President-Elect Trump to congratulate him on his victory. She accepted the results of the election and offered to help him and his team as they come back to the White House. Then she addressed the American people from Howard University, where she had gone to college years before. She walked out to a large crowd of cheering supporters with "Freedom" by Beyoncé playing on the speakers.

From the stage, Kamala gave one of the hardest speeches of her life. But even though it was hard, she talked about the joy and hope she had found during the campaign. She also spoke directly to the young people listening, letting them know that it's okay to lose and that losing doesn't mean giving up. She said: "Sometimes the fight takes a while. That doesn't mean we won't win. The important thing is, don't ever give up. Don't ever stop trying to make the world a better place. You have power, and don't you ever listen when anyone tells you something is impossible because it has never been done before. You have the capacity to do extraordinary good in the world."

While this wasn't the way she had dreamed the presidential election would turn out, Kamala's attempt to get to the White House in 2024 had come to an end. And while she didn't wind up becoming the first woman to be president, like

Hillary Clinton, she had helped pave the way for other women to try and, one day, succeed in becoming president of the United States.

HOW YOU CAN PERSIST

by Raakhee Mirchandani

If you want to bring impactful, purposeful, and powerful Kamala Harris energy into your life, there's lots you can do. Like Kamala, you have the ability to change the world, starting with your community. Here's how you can get started:

1. Speak up. If you see something that doesn't make sense, say something. If you notice something that isn't

working for people, do something. Your voice is your power.

2. Raise your hand. You may run for president one day, so you'll want to get some elections under your belt. Run for office in your school. Consider leadership positions in your community and in clubs, extracurricular activities, or sports teams.

3. Be an upstander. An upstander is someone who chooses to support someone who is being harmed by getting involved, not just watching an injustice happen.

4. Try a new recipe. Cooking can be creative, fun, and a way to bring people together. Try baking or cooking

something new. Then, share the finished food with friends and family. A family meal—or snack—is a great way to connect with loved ones.

5. Pronounce names correctly. Kamala's name is often mispronounced, sometimes purposely to be mean to her. Pronouncing people's names correctly is both respectful and important.

6. Serve your community. There are things in your hometown that are worth fighting for. And there are people right in your community who could use your help. Think about ways you can help your community grow and spend some time fighting for causes

you believe in.

7. Write a letter to an elected official. Is there something you wish your mayor, governor, senator, vice president, or president knew about? A letter is a great way to make your voice heard at all levels of government. You can find mailing addresses for elected officials on municipal or government websites. Ask a grown-up to help you!

8. Learn your family history and then ask your friends about their family history. Connecting with your own roots—and learning about those who came before you—is an important way to honor your family's journey. And listening to friends and neighbors talk about their

family's journey isn't just informative, it's fun, too!

9. Give a speech. Sign up for a speech contest or deliver a persuasive speech in your living room. It doesn't matter where you do it, but working on crafting a solid argument, with facts and stories mixed in, will help you give a speech that will convince others to take action.

10. Learn about the many women, specifically pioneering women of color such as Shirley Chisholm and Ida B. Wells or leaders such as Hillary Clinton and Geraldine Ferraro, who made significant cracks in the glass ceiling. Do school projects about them and

tell others about their contributions to American democracy.

11. Trust yourself. There are going to be times when people will count you out or try to convince you that you can't do something. You know that you are capable of big, hard things. You know that you are a change agent. So trust yourself and go forth and make this world a better place. I believe in you!

12. Join or organize a march. You can march in support of something you believe in or against something you disagree with. The right to peaceful assembly is guaranteed by the First Amendment to the Constitution of the United States. These amendments,

and the Constitution, are incredibly important to American democracy, and the more you know about them, the better.

13. Vote and volunteer. While you can't vote until you're eighteen years old, you can be a part of the democratic process well before that. Encourage the adults in your life to vote. Remind them of all those who fought for this important American right. You can also support candidates— or causes—through door knocking, postcard-writing campaigns, and making and hanging signs in your window. So grab a grown-up and get to it—America needs you!

Acknowledgments

....

My eleven-year-old daughter Satya—and Vice President Kamala Harris—have the same middle name. Devi. It was also my grandmother's name. Devi means goddess: the powerful, divine force that resides in all girls and women. I chose Devi as Satya's middle name because my grandmother was fierce and I wanted Satya to carry her ancestors' strength with her, wherever she went. I've often wondered what Kamala's mother, Shyamala Gopalan Harris, held in her heart when she chose her daughter's names.

Satya was seven years old during the 2020 Biden-Harris campaign, and the two of us spent a lot of time talking about "Devi energy" and how running for office definitely requires it! For me, being a Devi is being brave, serving your community, and standing up for others and for what you think is right. It's about action and participation and doing hard things for the greater good. Satya even dressed up like Vice President Harris for Halloween that year: suit, Converse, pearls, and all. We were both so inspired by her work and her words and were proud to see a Black and Indian woman at the highest levels of the United States government.

Running for president also requires Devi energy. And watching Vice President Harris make the fearless, patriotic, and courageous decision to run for president of the United States—to serve and represent all Americans—made me emotional. It still does.

I really wanted to write this book about Kamala Harris for young readers, because Satya and I have been obsessed with the She Persisted series for years, learning so much together about so many inspiring women who've used their voices for good. A huge, heartfelt thank-you to my agent, Liza Fleissig, for being my boldest champion and changing my life. You have made so many of my dreams come true, including this book.

Thank you to my editors—and friends—Talia Benamy and Jill Santopolo, for the world-changing work you both do to diversify bookshelves. Working with you is a master class in being a change agent, and I feel incredibly blessed to be on your team. And to the entire Philomel team, including Alexandra Boiger, Jessica W. Clark, Ellice Lee, Lori Thorn, Gaby Corzo, Sola Akinlana, Marinda Valenti, and Krista Ahlberg, thank you for all the care you've poured into this project. Your precision and open hearts are truly appreciated. And to Chelsea Clinton: You are an example of what is possible when women lead and create. I am so proud to be part of the persisterhood. Thank you for making this space for so many of us.

My village is a bustling, supportive place. Thank you to my coven, Emily, Cristin, Rachel, and Nora, the most democracy-loving ladies I've ever met. And to my core crew: Elidia, Neve, Aman, Haseena, Cristy, Supriya, Nisha, and Akruti. Thank you for cheering me on as I worked on this manuscript over the summer. Having women like you all in my corner is the most empowering feeling in the world.

Everything begins and ends with family for me. Thank

you to my parents, Jyoti (Deena) and Pirkash, for their relentless pursuit of the American dream and their endless belief in me. And to my mother-in-law, Surjit Kaur, for all your support.

And to my husband, Agan, and daughter, Satya, the moon and the stars of my life: Thank you both for always making me feel like the sun. With you both, I am creative, capable, limitless, and worthy. The three of us share a union that feels like it's been built over lifetimes, and I want nothing more than to read and write, curled up on the sofa, next to you both, for decades to come. We did it, team!

Finally, to those who have run for office—in my home sweet Hoboken, that's you, Mayor Bhalla and Councilwoman Jabbour. And of course nationally, Vice President Harris and Secretary Hillary Clinton. Thank you for showing us what it looks like to serve our community— and the people—with clarity of purpose. It's this selfless dedication to America, and our collective future, that will inspire the next generation of ceiling smashers.

∽ References ∾

Anderson, Kirsten. *Who Is Kamala Harris?*
New York: Penguin Workshop, 2021.

Bailey, Megan. "Between Two Worlds: Black
Women and the Fight for Voting Rights,"
National Park Service. US Department of
the Interior. nps.gov/articles/black-women
-and-the-fight-for-voting-rights.htm.

"The Civil Rights Act of 1964," United
States Senate. https://www.senate.gov
/artandhistory/history/civil_rights
/CivilRights_CloturePrimaryDocs.htm.

Dixon, Liwag Christine. "The Untold Truth of Kamala Harris." The List, July 31, 2020. thelist.com/232185/the-untold-truth-of -kamala-harris.

"Elections and Voting." The White House. whitehouse.gov/about-the-white-house/our -government/elections-and-voting.

Grant, Tonya K. *National Geographic Kids: Kamala Harris*. Washington, D.C.: National Geographic Kids, 2022.

Haines, Errin. "Kamala Harris Wants America to Turn Protest Into Policy. Is She the One to Make It Happen?" *Washington Post*, June 19, 2020. washingtonpost.com/politics /2020/06/19/there-was-this-tool-that-they -had-figured-out-was-powerful-kamala-harris -working-system-justice.

Halper, Evan. "A Political Awakening: How Howard University Shaped Kamala Harris' Identity." *Los Angeles Times*, March 19, 2019. latimes.com/politics/la-na-pol-kamala-harris -howard-university-20190319-story.html.

Harris, Kamala. *Superheroes Are Everywhere.* New York: Philomel, 2019.

Harris, Kamala. *The Truths We Hold: An American Journey.* New York: Penguin Books, 2019.

"'I Won't Be the Last': Kamala Harris, First Woman Elected US Vice-President, Accepts Place in History." *The Guardian*, November 8, 2020. theguardian.com/us-news/2020 /nov/07/kamala-harris-victory-speech-first -woman-vice-president.

"Legal Highlight: The Civil Rights Act of

1964." Office of the Assistant Secretary for Administration and Management, US Department of Labor. dol.gov/agencies/oasam/civil-rights-center/statutes/civil-rights-act-of-1964.

"Not All Women Gained the Vote in 1920," American Experience. PBS. July 6, 2020. pbs.org/wgbh/americanexperience/features/vote-not-all-women-gained-right-to-vote-in-1920.

"Plaintiffs in California's Prop. 8 Case Wed in SF, LA," ABC7. June 29, 2013. abc7.com/archive/9156079.

Rani, Sharma Rikha. "The Woman Who Led Kamala Harris to This Moment." *The Atlantic*, October 25, 2020. theatlantic.com/politics/archive/2020/10/kamala-harris-mother-shyamala-gopalan/616374.

Ring, Trudy. "How Pro-LGBTQ+ is Kamala Harris?" *The Advocate*, August 21, 2024. advocate.com/politics/kamala-harris-lgbtq -record#toggle-gdpr.

Sedensky, Matt. "For Harris, Memories of a Warrior Mother Guide Her Campaign." Associated Press, May 11, 2019, apnews.com /article/0b55116cc42c4a80b3a34b5080e98e40.

Walsh, Joan. "Kamala Harris Has Been Here Before." *The Nation*, July 29, 2019. thenation .com/article/archive/kamala-harris-terence -hallinan-willie-brown/tnamp.

RAAKHEE MIRCHANDANI is a journalist, children's book author, activist, and mom. Her work has appeared in *Elle*, *Glamour*, *The Wall Street Journal*, *Redbook*, *HuffPo*, *Moneyish*, the *New York Post*, the *New York Daily News*, and the *Boston Herald*, and her books include *She Persisted: Kalpana Chawla*, *Kamala Raised Her Hand*, *Journey to the Stars*, *Hair Twins*, *Super Satya Saves the Day*, and *My Diwali Light*. When she isn't writing or working on her podcast, Raakhee is either organizing her bookshelves, running races to raise money for the fight against pediatric cancer, or styling her very curly hair with new oils and potions. She lives in Hoboken, New Jersey, with her husband and daughter.

You can visit Raakhee Mirchandani online at
RaakstarWrites.com
or follow her on Instagram
@RaakstarWrites

JESSICA W. CLARK grew up in Rexburg, Idaho, and earned her BFA in illustration from BYU-Idaho. Jessica spent several years in Europe, where she discovered a love of architecture, photography, and art history. Now Jessica lives near Dallas, Texas, with her husband and five children. Having five children has helped her keep the magic in her life, and she likes to transfer those everyday magical memories into her illustrations.

Photo credit: Christina Freeman

You can visit Jessica W. Clark online at
JessicaWClark.com
or follow her on Instagram
@JessicaWClarkIllustration

CHELSEA CLINTON is the author of the #1 *New York Times* bestseller *She Persisted: 13 American Women Who Changed the World*; *She Persisted Around the World: 13 Women Who Changed History*; *She Persisted in Sports: American Olympians Who Changed the Game*; *She Persisted in Science: Brilliant Women Who Made a Difference*; *Don't Let Them Disappear: 12 Endangered Species Across the Globe*; *Welcome to the Big Kids Club*; *It's Your World: Get Informed, Get Inspired & Get Going!*; *Start Now!: You Can Make a Difference*; with Hillary Clinton, *Grandma's Gardens* and *Gutsy Women*; and, with Devi Sridhar, *Governing Global Health: Who Runs the World and Why?* She is also the Vice Chair of the Clinton Foundation, where she works on many initiatives, including those that help empower the next generation of leaders. She lives in New York City with her husband, Marc, and their children.

You can follow Chelsea Clinton on Twitter
@ChelseaClinton
or on Facebook at
facebook.com/chelseaclinton

ALEXANDRA BOIGER has illustrated nearly twenty picture books, including the She Persisted books by Chelsea Clinton; the popular Tallulah series by Marilyn Singer; and the Max and Marla books, which she also wrote. Originally from Munich, Germany, she now lives outside of San Francisco, California, with her husband, Andrea, daughter, Vanessa, and two cats, Luiso and Winter.

Photo credit: Vanessa Blasich

You can visit Alexandra Boiger online at
alexandraboiger.com
or follow her on Instagram
@alexandra_boiger

She Persisted series

2 04